Floored! Supercars

BUGATTI

By Jennifer Colby

45th Parallel Press

Published in the United States of America by Cherry Lake Publishing Group
Ann Arbor, Michigan
www.cherrylakepublishing.com

Reading Adviser: Beth Walker Gambro, MS Ed., Reading Consultant, Yorkville, IL
Book Designer: Jen Wahi

Photo Credits: © Max Earey/Shutterstock, cover, 1; © khatmi marwen/Shutterstock, 4; © supermodel/Shutterstock, 6, 7; © 360b/Shutterstock, 8; © Skblzz1/Wikimedia, 10; © The History Collection/Alamy Stock Photo, 11; © supermodel/Shutterstock, 12, 14, 17, 18, 19, 22, 29, 31; © Oleksandr Grechin/Shutterstock, 13; © classic topcar/Shutterstock, 14; © Heritage Image Partnership Ltd/Alamy Stock Photo, 20, 30; © Steve Allen Travel Photography/Alamy Stock Photo, 21; © Artoholics/Shutterstock, 23; © Mike Mareen/Shutterstock, 24; © Alexandru Nika/Shutterstock, 27; © Massimo Campanari/Shutterstock, 30; © dimcars/Shutterstock, 31.

Copyright © 2023 by Cherry Lake Publishing Group

All rights reserved. No part of this book may be reproduced or utilized in any form or by any means without written permission from the publisher.

45th Parallel Press is an imprint of Cherry Lake Publishing Group.

Library of Congress Cataloging-in-Publication Data

Names: Colby, Jennifer, 1971- author.
Title: Bugatti / by Jennifer Colby.
Description: Ann Arbor, Michigan : Cherry Lake Publishing, [2022] | Series: Floored! Supercars
Identifiers: LCCN 2022005330 | ISBN 9781668909522 (hardcover) | ISBN 9781668911129 (paperback) | ISBN 9781668912713 (ebook) | ISBN 9781668914304 (pdf)
Subjects: LCSH: Bugatti automobile--Juvenile literature. | Sports cars--Juvenile literature.
Classification: LCC TL215.B82 C58 2022 | DDC 629.222/2--dc23/eng/20220209
LC record available at https://lccn.loc.gov/2022005330

Printed in the United States of America by
Corporate Graphics

ABOUT THE AUTHOR:

Jennifer Colby is a school librarian in Ann Arbor, Michigan. She does not drive a supercar, but she likes going to auto shows to see what they look like.

Table of Contents

CHAPTER 1:
What Are Supercars? 5

CHAPTER 2:
Bugatti History 9

CHAPTER 3:
Bugatti Racing 15

CHAPTER 4:
Bugatti Today 25

TIMELINE OF A LEGEND 30

FIND OUT MORE 32

GLOSSARY 32

INDEX 32

One place to see a Bugatti supercar is at an auto show.

CHAPTER 1
What Are Supercars?

Cars get us where we need to go. We drive them to school and work. We drive them to the grocery store or a friend's house. If we need to go someplace, a car can get us there. But some people want a car that is more than a way to get around. They want a car with high **performance** and **luxury** features. Performance is how well something works. Luxury means great comfort. These car owners want to drive a **supercar**.

A supercar is a sports car. It is designed to provide a high-level driving experience. Drivers of supercars expect excellent **acceleration**, **handling**, and **maneuvering**. Acceleration is the act of moving faster. Handling is the way a car moves when it is driven. Maneuvering is a skillful way of moving. Supercars are also known for their unique looks. You might see one of these eye-catching cars and admire it.

Have you seen a Bugatti driving down the road? If so, then you have seen a supercar! What makes these cars so special?

Let's find out more about Bugattis.

Bugattis are known for their artistic design.

The Bugatti logo includes founder Ettore Bugatti's initials.

CHAPTER 2
Bugatti History

Bugatti is a well-known supercar manufacturer. The company has been making performance cars for more than 100 years. Italian engineer Ettore Bugatti started the company in 1909. Bugatti is known for its designs and early successes in racing.

Born in 1881, Ettore Bugatti was a **pioneer** of car design. A pioneer creates new looks, styles, and methods. He was surrounded by artists. His grandfather, Giovanni Luigi Bugatti, was a well-known architect. His father, Carlo Bugatti, designed jewelry, furniture, and musical instruments. His uncle, Giovanni Segantini, was a famous painter. And his younger brother, Rembrandt Bugatti, was a sculptor.

In 1898, Bugatti designed the "Bugatti Type 1," a motorized tricycle. He started his own automobile manufacturing company called Automobile E. Bugatti.

Bugatti died in 1947. In 2000, he was **inducted** into the Automotive Hall of Fame. Inducted means added. He was one of the most famous car designers of the 20th century.

Ettore Bugatti's first automotive design was a motorized tricycle like this.

Ettore Bugatti in 1926.

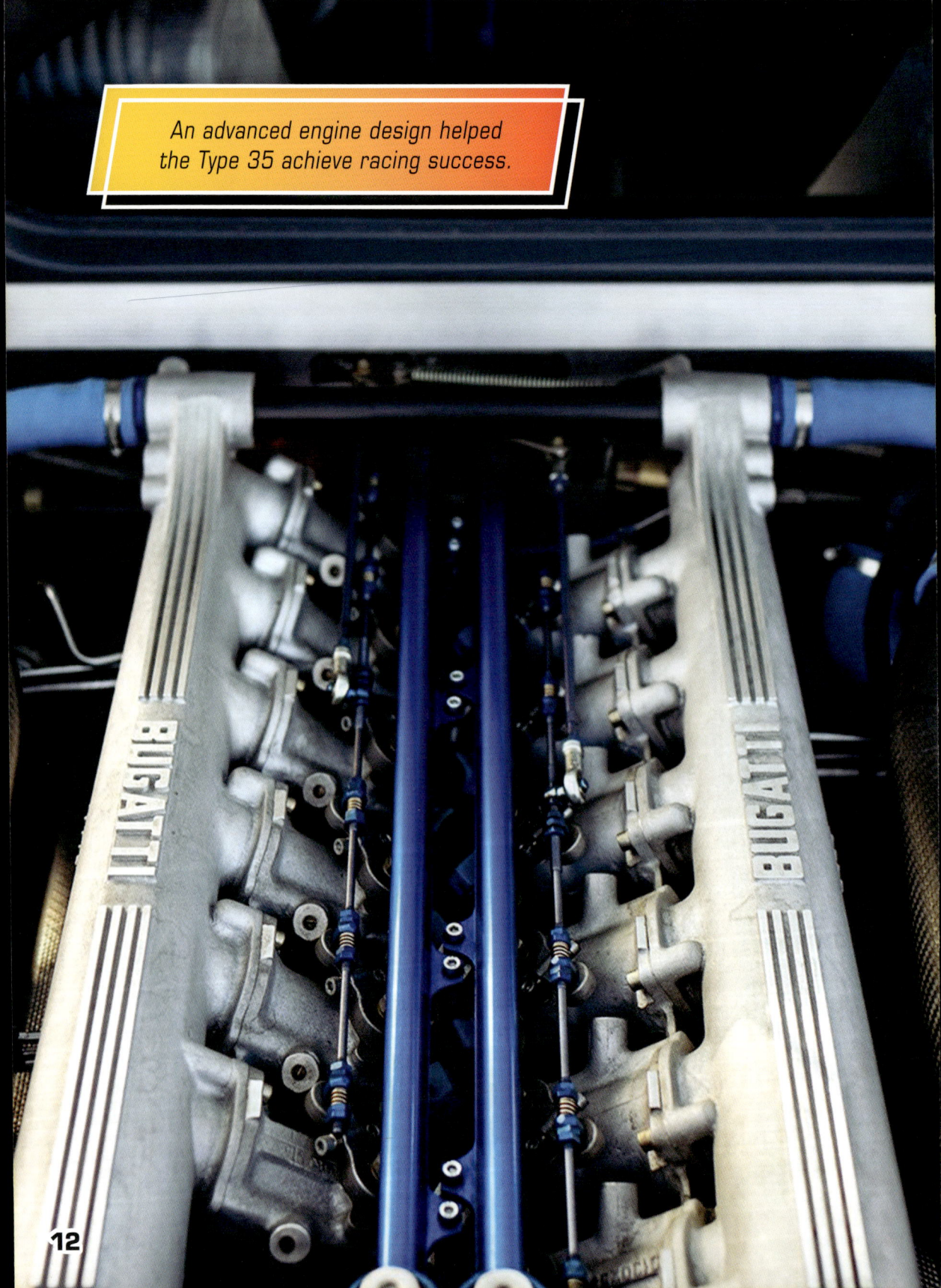

An advanced engine design helped the Type 35 achieve racing success.

Behind the Wheel

Czechoslovakian racer Eliška Junková-Khásová was the first woman to win a **Grand Prix** event. Grand Prix races are run on closed roads or on courses designed to be like real-life roadways. She was also known as Elisabeth Junek. She started racing professionally in 1923. People called her the "queen of the steering wheel."

In 1928, Junek drove a Bugatti Type 35 in the Targa Florio race in Sicily, Italy. The race over mountain roads was very dangerous. On her final lap, she had mechanical troubles. She finished in fifth place.

A Bugatti owner complained that his car did not start easily on cold mornings. Bugatti said, "Sir! If you can afford a Type 35, you can surely afford a heated garage!"

CHAPTER 3
Bugatti Racing

The first Bugatti to win a Grand Prix race was a Type 13. Ernest Friderich was the Bugatti's driver. The Type 13 was smaller than many race cars of the time. But it made up for its size with its great steering and handling. Its top speed was almost 78 miles (125.5 kilometers) per hour. Today, that may not sound fast. However, back then, the most popular road car was the Ford Model T. Its top speed was only about 40 miles (64 km) per hour!

In 1921, the Type 13 won the top 4 spots in the Italian Grand Prix. The mid-1920s brought the Bugatti Type 35. It won more than 2,000 races between 1924 and 1930.

The Type 35 performed well because of its new features, such as its powerful **crankshaft**. A crankshaft connects a vehicle's engine to the wheels and helps turn them. The Type 35 also had 2 **carburetors**. Carburetors are engine parts that mix air with liquid fuel. The extra carburetor helped the engine run smoothly. The car moved at speeds of up to 118 miles (190 km) per hour!

Bugatti designed cars for top speeds. A Bugatti owner once questioned the car's braking ability. Bugatti replied, "I make my cars to go, not stop!"

The sleek interior of a Bugatti.

Buyers of the Chiron Super Sport 300+ can prepare for driving the ultra-fast car on a test track.

In 1929, a Bugatti Type 35B won the first Monaco Grand Prix in Monte Carlo. The driver was British racer William Grover-Williams. Grover-Williams set the top lap speed of 2 minutes and 15 seconds.

William Grover-Williams drives a Bugatti Type 35B in the Monaco Grand Prix in 1929.

The Bugatti Veyron's style and performance make it a sought-after car.

Only 30 models of the Chiron Super Sport 300+ were made. Each was painted with orange racing stripes.

AT TOP SPEED

- In 2013, the Bugatti Veyron Grand Sport Vitesse became the fastest road car in production. It had a top speed of 254 miles (409 km) per hour.

- In 2019, a Bugatti Chiron Super Sport 300+ was the first car to break the speed barrier of 300 miles (483 km) per hour.

- The super-powered engine of the Chiron Super Sport 300+ is nicknamed "Thor."

- In 2021, a Veyron raced a French fighter jet. The car was winning until the jet took off from the runway.

Which Bugatti is your favorite?

CHAPTER 4
Bugatti Today

Bugatti car owners expect perfection. All Bugattis are custom designed, from the paint color to the brakes. Buyers can choose nearly every exterior look of a Bugatti. This attention to detail means that almost every Bugatti is unique.

The Bugatti Chiron has more than 1,800 individual parts. It is hand-built by highly trained **technicians**. A technician is someone who works with machines. It takes about 8 months to build and deliver a Bugatti.

Bugattis are the most expensive cars available today. All current models cost millions of dollars. The Bugatti's high-quality parts contribute to its big price tag.

The Veyron engine is powered by 4 **turbochargers**. Turbochargers are devices that compress, or squeeze, air. Each one costs $6,400! But that's not all. The 2 air coolers that connect to the turbochargers are $9,000 each.

The expense of a Bugatti does not end with its purchase. Maintaining a Bugatti costs about $50,000 per year. A new set of tires costs about $38,000! Average car owners might pay $50 for an oil change on their car. Changing the Bugatti's fluids once each year costs $25,000. But the cost of these cars is the price for driving a superior performance machine.

Bugattis are among the most stylish cars on the road. You can recognize a Bugatti by its horseshoe-shaped grill. This unique feature honors the company's design history.

In 2019, Bugatti introduced a new one-off model, the La Voiture Noire. The La Voiture Noire is extra special because only one will ever be made! Its price was listed at $13.4 million. But it's said that the buyer paid more than $18 million for it.

A version of La Voiture Noire was first displayed at the 2019 Geneva Motor Show.

Cost of Ownership

MODEL	PRICE
2021 Honda CRV	$25,350
2021 Ford Escape	$25,555
2021 Chevy Suburban	$52,300

MODEL	PRICE
2005 Bugatti Veyron	$1.9 Million
2021 Bugatti Chiron	$3 Million
2019 Bugatti Divo	$5.7 Million
2020 Bugatti Centodieci	$8.9 Million
2019 Bugatti La Voiture Noire	$13.4 Million (estimated)

No one knows for sure who bought the car in 2021. Bugatti does not make this information public. But the new owner is most likely a well-known World Cup soccer player. And it is not his first Bugatti!

For more than 100 years, Bugattis have been known for their distinctive design.

Timeline of a Legend

- First Grand Prix victory at Le Mans

1920

- Type 35 is produced

1929

1924

1998

- Volkswagen Group purchases Bugatti brand

- First Monaco Grand Prix victory

1909

- Founding of Bugatti

30

- Bugatti celebrates 100 years

2009

- Bugatti breaks the 300 mph (483 kph) barrier

2019

2021

- Bugatti produces the most expensive new car at $13.4 million

2016

- Chiron is produced

2005

- Veyron is produced

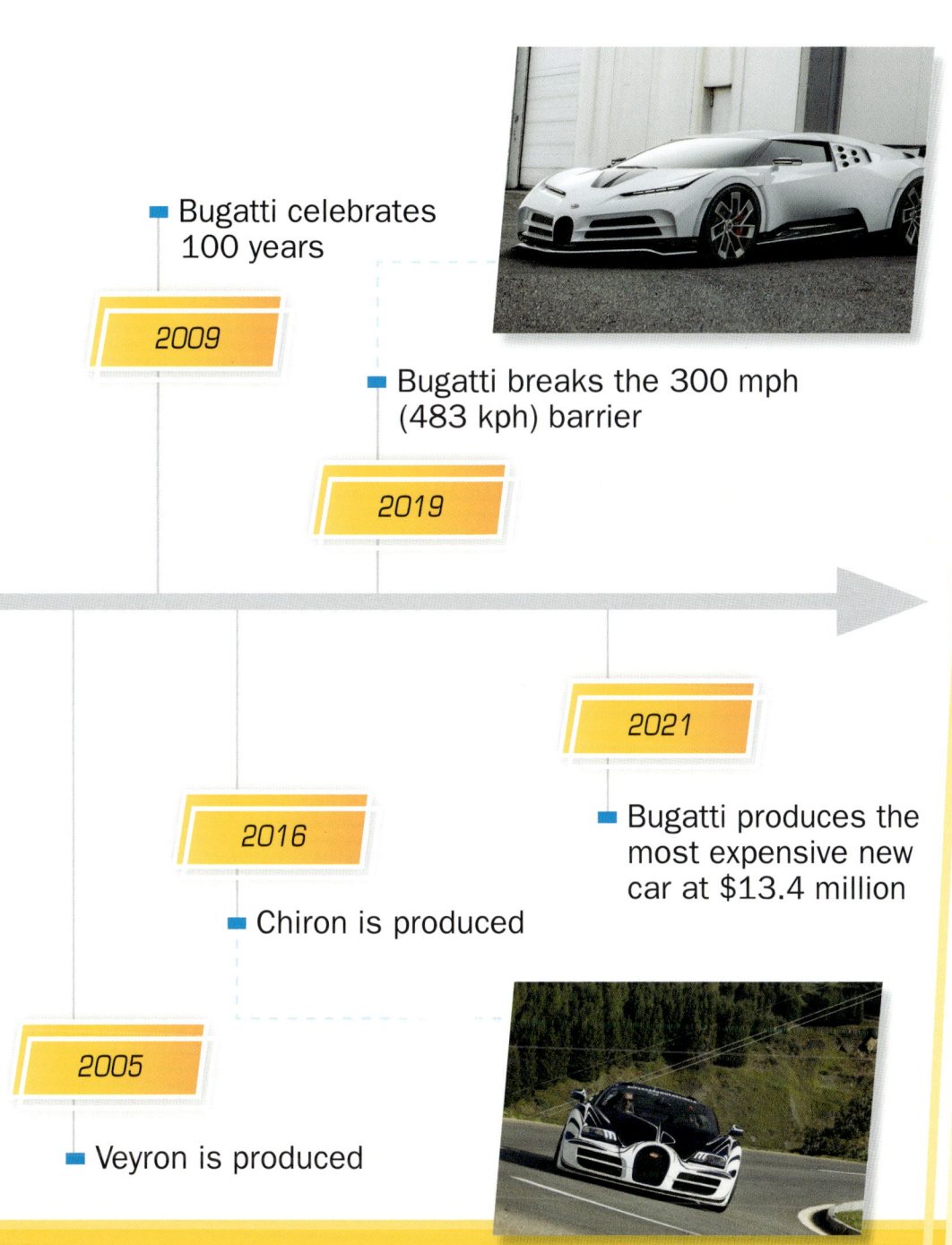

Find Out More

BOOKS

Garstecki, Julia, and Stephanie Derkovitz. *Bugatti Chiron*. North Mankato, MN: Black Rabbit Books, 2020.

Oachs, Emily Rose. *Bugatti Chiron*. Minneapolis, MN: Bellwether Media, 2018.

WEBSITES

Bugatti—Chronicles
https://www.bugatti.com/brand/history/chronicles

Kiddle—Sportscar Facts for Kids
https://kids.kiddle.co/Sportscar

Glossary

acceleration (ik-seh-luh-RAY-shuhn) the act of moving faster

carburetors (KAR-buh-ray-tuhrz) parts in an internal combustion engine that mix air with fuel

crankshaft (KRANK-shaft) a long metal part that connects an engine to the wheels and helps turn them

Grand Prix (GRAND PREE) European car race run on closed roads or on courses designed to be like roadways

handling (HAND-ling) the way a car moves when it is driven

inducted (in-DUK-tuhd) recognized as a contributor to an organization or group

luxury (LUHK-shuh-ree) great comfort and wealth

maneuvering (muh-NOO-vuh-ring) moving in a skillful way

performance (puh-FOHR-muhns) how well something functions or works

pioneer (pye-uh-NIHR) person who creates or develops new ideas and methods

supercar (SOO-puhr-kar) sports car designed for a high-level driving experience

technicians (tek-NIH-shuhnz) people whose jobs relate to the use of machines

turbochargers (TUHR-boh-char-juhrz) devices that compress air into a carburetor

Index

B
Bugatti
  acceleration, 5
  carburetors, 16
  crankshaft, 16
  engine, 12, 16, 23, 25
  handling, 5, 15
  history, 9
  logo, 8
  maneuvering, 5
  racing, 9, 12–13, 15, 22
  technicians, 25
  timeline, 30–31
Bugatti, Ettore, 8–11, 16

E
engineer, 9

G
Grand Prix, 13, 15–16, 20, 30
Grover-Williams, William, 20

J
Junek, Elisabeth, 13

S
supercar, 4–6, 9,

T
turbochargers, 26

W
wheels, 16